ID0850768

Also by Sylvie Baumgartel

Song of Songs

PINK

PINK

SYLVIE
BAUMGARTEL

FARRAR, STRAUS AND GIROUX / NEW YORK

Farrar, Straus and Giroux
120 Broadway, New York 10271

Grateful acknowledgment is made to the publications in which versions of the
following poems originally appeared: *Harvard Review*: "Painting," "Pregnancy";
The Nation: "Algeria"; *The New York Review of Books*: "Etiquette"; *The Paris
Review*: "Caprice," "The Fortune Teller," "Gramercy Park," "Picnic with Mom,"
"Pink," "The Ponte Vecchio"; *Ploughshares*: "Stiletto," "Volterra"; *Raritan*:
"Girl"; *Subtropics*: "Black," *"Cum Clave,"* "The Hamburg Sisters in Nebraska,"
"The Mission Bell," "The Washing"; *The Unprofessionals* (Penguin, 2015):
"Gramercy Park"; and *Virginia Quarterly Review*: "Mothers," "Pink."

Word definitions in these poems come from
The Oxford English Dictionary twenty-volume set.

Library of Congress Cataloging-in-Publication Data
Names: Baumgartel, Sylvie, author.
Title: Pink / Sylvie Baumgartel.
Description: First edition. | New York : Farrar, Straus and Giroux, 2021.
Identifiers: LCCN 2020042789 | ISBN 9780374601201 (hardcover)
Subjects: LCGFT: Poetry.
Classification: LCC PS3602.A9645 P56 2021 | DDC 811/.6—dc23
LC record available at https://lccn.loc.gov/2020042789

Designed by Crisis

Our books may be purchased in bulk for promotional, educational, or
business use. Please contact your local bookseller or the Macmillan
Corporate and Premium Sales Department at 1-800-221-7945, extension
5442, or by email at MacmillanSpecialMarkets@macmillan.com.

www.fsgbooks.com
www.twitter.com/fsgbooks
www.facebook.com/fsgbooks

1 3 5 7 9 10 8 6 4 2

For Nancy & for Virginia

CONTENTS

PINK

THE WASHING

Mothers & daughters have secrets.
I knead the delicates, she needs the secrets.
We don't separate the lights from the darks.
The pink lines bleed into the white lies.

When they cleaned the Sistine Chapel,
The fig leaves were removed
To expose the original genitals.
But the eyes' dark pupils were lost.

CUM CLAVE

The night sky on the vaulted
Ceiling of the Sistine Chapel
Was hacked off star by gold star
For Michelangelo to make the
World from scratch.

I think I remember a serene birth.
My pink body & the blue pulsing rope
Cut by a masked man.
My mother's long thighs
Painted in blood & water as
My father's blue eyes looked first
Into the universe of my mouth.

I can't see the stop-motion
Lions hunting in the Lascaux cave.
They are being saved
From my breath;
They are being preserved
For future bodies to destroy.
But I want to breathe on those
Lions & watch them run.

It's my skin, my sweat & my breath
That destroys Michelangelo's ceiling too.
You locked my mouth closed with your
Finger key in your Porsche in Rome
Until I nodded, *Yes, you own me.*
Every time I remember you, I alter you.

Michelangelo made his God a man
& gave his Moses horns.
It's the wet of my body &
My breath that destroys you too.

BLACK

God is a brain on the ceiling
Of the Sistine Chapel.
Michelangelo created the end
Of the world with divine God
In the shape of a human brain
Complete with glands & brainstem.
Our reptile & our please & thank you.
Our sight inside seeing & that which
Grows our body hair & smell.
Michelangelo destroyed almost all
Of his drawings in a bonfire.
Probably so we couldn't know how much
Work went into his work.
A bonfire comes from a *bone fire*.
There was a thief who stole
A Gutenberg Bible from a Harvard library
So he could read the *original truth*.
He stole the book all dressed in black.
He became a porn star because he
Could put his penis in his mouth.
He said that swallowing his own sperm
Was the creation of eternity & he
Desired to make the world anew.
He loved the color black the most
Because it's infinity.

FAMILY

My father watches me climb
A pyramid and get beheaded.

Westinghouse washing machine says
Doctor doctor doctor
On the wash cycle and
Good cheese good cheese good cheese
On the rinse cycle
In a squeaky voice like a rat.

My mother scatters wildflower
Seeds in her new perm.
At night she knits a green acrylic dress.
She's waiting for the stones to tumble down
The mountain and smash the house.
She's waiting for another baby to save yesterday.

My mother combs out of her hair:
Lutefisk, a broom, a reindeer.
Wooden shoes, shortbread.
She braids me in, combs me out.

How do you make a brother?
At night we press our bodies into our dark sleeping bodies.

I thought my brother was for me.
I climbed into his crib and tried to eat him.

Don't ever do that again.
But I did.
I painted my toenails pink with stolen polish.
My father drove a truck he called Ghost.
I tried to eat my brother again but he was too big.
Ronald Reagan was very upset about the shuttle exploding.

My grandmother said,
Don't go to Smith and don't get fat.
Everything she saved for seventy years
I lost in twenty minutes.

PREGNANCY

I feel numb.
Everything in me is
Going somewhere else.
Even my words
Before I speak them
Go into the pumping, dark
Blood that feeds my
Part parasite,
Part god, baby boy.

I can smell it.
Piero's pregnant Madonna
& I vomit together
On the rock outside.
I wonder if what paintings
Really want is to reproduce.
A baby of their own.

PAINTING

The most beautiful white is poison.
Yellow is the gallbladder of an ox.
Sienna is the mountain.
Fra Angelico ground pigment
Out of Scripture.

I trim my hair & I emerge.

Piero della Francesca did not
Paint Saint Apollonia
Strapped to a tree in a forest—
A furious mob yanking out
Her teeth with golden pliers.
Or roped to a plank, her blond
Hair wrenched, like Fouquet did.

Instead, a passionless Apollonia—
A single tooth poised,
Plucked by her own hand.
Blank look in her eyes
As if nothing ever happened.

I'm the girl projected;
I'm the girl unprotected.
I am Apollonia.

THE MISSION BELL

In our country's oldest mission church,
Built atop a sacred Native settlement,
There is a bell. One at human
Height, one you can touch. Too heavy
For the adobe tower, it tumbled and fell
And for years lay in the graveyard before
Being brought inside to live on the floor.
It's made from kettles, hammers,
Jewelry, iron, bronze, lead, silver, gold.
Any metal the people had in Spain to throw in to
Make the bell, to make this bell
To help expel the Moors. The bell was taken
By ship to Mexico, then carried by cart up here to
Santa Fe and placed in the Mission of San Miguel.
The church proudly proclaims that it has the
Sweetest peal on earth because it was made with
Love and sacrifice. This bell to ring,
This bell to claim Spain as Christian now,
Not Moorish anymore, and here to claim
That this sacred earth is not Native anymore.
Love and sacrifice.
I was surprised by the alleged pedophile priest
Who walked over to me and shot his blue eyes
Through my child and asked if he could touch my son.

In Argentina there is a school for the deaf.
The priests didn't teach the boys to sign, and they
Destroyed all the letters written to the outside
For help. The priests who got caught said
They thought they could get away with it
Because the boys couldn't hear each other
Scream.

LAND OF FIRE

You can't get the shape of my hips
Out of your head.
My hips, or hips from a black
& white photo you saw long ago
Of a girl Gauguin would have done (or did).

I'm thinking of the photo from Tierra del Fuego
Of a girl dressed in the skin of a seal,
Smoke curling up behind her
In the black & white sky.
She was bounty hunted for two
Pounds sterling per pair of ears.

I don't know what I see when I look at you.
You see me as a girl in a grass skirt with fleshy hips.
I saw you coming, the way
The Native Americans saw
The ships they couldn't see.

Chatwin tells the story of an African man
Who saw an elephant from a distance
For the first time & thought it was an ant.

SONG FROM LONG AGO

I crawl inside my father & lie
Peeking out his eyes.
My brown is glassed in blue.

THE BAKER'S DAUGHTER

As a child, you taught me
To glaze your glass with only
The breath of vermouth
& to spray only a faint breath
Of Chanel N° 5 on your coat.

You drew lines on my
Arms with black ink & a ruler.
This much of my arm on the table
For a midday meal,
& *only this much* for supper.
You were the baker's daughter.

You took me to see the white bears.
We walked on the ice of the Pole
In fur hats next to men with guns.

You asked me to cover my eyes
When we saw a woman undress, exposing
Her tits for Harrison Ford.

You asked me again to cover my eyes
When I ran the sponge

Over scars drawn into you long & sharp.
Your suddenly gnarled, bony &
Breastless body.

Raphael too loved
A baker's daughter.
He painted her holding her
Hand over her breast,
Not wanting us to see
The growth that was going to kill her.

THE HAMBURG SISTERS IN NEBRASKA

We don't talk about *that*.
We make fruitcakes.
We love our husbands like cardboard.
We keep our nails trimmed close.
The skin under our eyes is like
Drowned moons.
The skin between our eyes is
Gathered like skirt pleats.
We hide our purple nipples.
We forget our language.
You can't speak it anymore anyway.
We crochet dresses from bakery string.
We stink of candy grease.
We collect dolls with soft cloth
Bodies & hard limbs.
At church they say to us:
You stink of doughnuts, poor idiots.
The folks who eat our
Doughnuts call us "hamburgers."
They think that's funny.
Moving from South Dakota to Nebraska,
To Iowa. Back to Nebraska.
Town to town after the bakery fails.

The children stink of bakery grease.
We can't wash off that smell
Even when bathed in kerosene.
We press violets in dictionaries.
We starve in the basement
During a tornado.

STALK

The main stem,
A woody core.

A bit of straw,
The stipe of an ovary.

A slender part connecting
The animal to the organ.

The shank of a hawk,
The upright of a ladder,

The shaft of a chimney,
The stem of a wine glass.

An appendage to halter.
Walking softly & stealthily

To track prey unnoticed
Until within range

Of the hunted animal
For the purpose of the kill.

STILETTO

What happens to good girls?
They get presents.
What happens to bad girls?
They get tied up & locked in the closet.

A stiletto was first a pen,
Then a dagger,
Now a heel.
Caravaggio's Medusa was painted on a shield.
The painting itself is an object of warfare.
I wear purple marks from you on my
Eyes & hips.

Medusa's head is full of tin
From pots & pans & knives
Thrown into the molten bronze because
Cellini was feverish & threw in his
Kitchen to finish his sculpture.

I'm the girl projected;
I'm the girl unprotected.
My head too is full of the kitchen.
My head too is full of knives.

RED BALL, BLUE BOY

This bird is plump,
Lying dead on the kitchen floor.
My black spooky cat killed it.
The soft, glossy, pink curl
Of intestines, the scarlet bright
Wet of its heart, its blood,
Punctured by the spooky cat bite.
I love this bird. It is gray & brown
With a red-feathered breast.
It is surrounded by downy silver
Feathers. Its feet are curled.
When I was eight, I watched
A five-year-old boy drown
In a hotel swimming pool.
There were lots of us kids there,
Playing with a red rubber ball.
Then we saw the boy.
Floating, back to the sky,
Arms out. We turned him over
& he was blue & dead.
Adults grabbed him, did CPR.
His parents had been away at the bar.
The blue boy, splayed out

On his aqua cross.
His brown skinny legs
On the ambulance gurney
Looked like living legs, like
He was about to get up & run.
The massacred bird on the
Floor is full of stillness.
My five eyes begin to open.

GIRL

The best brown & black pigments for paint
Come from the dead.
Mummy Brown, Ivory Black, Bone Black.
Pliny the Elder said that
Painters have been known to dig up
Charred materials from graves.
Paintings have literally been alive.

Keep your sunny side up & your dirty side down,
My grandmother told me.
But I didn't listen.
I shine sunshine in the dirt;
I dig up my dead & make things.
She must have forgotten that the
Goddess of war & the goddess of
Poetry are one & the same.

A Roman Briton skeleton was just
Discovered buried facedown.
His tongue had been cut out.
Inside his mouth was a perfectly carved
Tongue made of thin stone.
What did he say or what were they
Afraid he was going to say?

Sometimes it's the man I love who
Unleashes the lightning in my hips
& sometimes it's God who does it.
Feel this, I'm doing it.
I'm a fierce fighter for good things.
I do it, I show you.
It's our decay that binds us & reminds us.

A master butcher doesn't ever need
To sharpen her blade.
She slices through the space in a body
Without touching the flesh.
I don't know how to do that;
I leave marks.

I am clean & sweet.
This is rage inside out.
I like women who do hard things.
Wendy Maldonado smashed in her husband's
Skull with a hammer while he slept.
Martha Stewart made a fortune
Baking simple cakes
& Saint Apollonia had her
Teeth ripped out with golden pliers.
I am her teeth I put back in.
The man without a tongue is speaking.

ETIQUETTE

I go to Spain to see where my rules come from.
The nuns feed me the soft gray brains of sheep.
My brain clenches like a fist.
I am sweet & violent.
I like to make things &
I like to break things.

Up the stairs before a man, down after.
I please you, I fear you.
This is a jam spoon, this is a honey spoon.
Into an elevator before a man, speak after.
It's this fork for fish, & that fork for cake.
I trip over my tongue.

I delicately remove the egg-yolk-orange
Stamens from the Casablanca lilies
So the pollen doesn't fall
Onto the tablecloth & stain it.
I set the table for tea.
I like discipline.
I like Goya's nightmares.
I have chairs on my head
& chairs coming out of my mouth.

Lucas Cranach the Elder painted
Lucretia's shame over & over & over.
He showed us Lucretia with her
Hips cocked, bald pubis, old-looking face.
Poised, holding the dagger about
To pierce her own heart.
The prince who snuck into her room
To rape her first awoke her
By gently washing her belly
With warm water & a cloth.

TEACHERS

At Santa Fe Prep, my chemistry
Teacher made me an offer when I
Was getting a C: *Pull up your shirt*
And let me touch your tits and
You will get an A.
I declined his offer and told
The headmaster. He said, "Can
You blame him?" And that was that.
In college it was my piano teacher
And a literature professor who made
Similar offers though my
Grades were good.
When I was young, in fifth grade,
My teacher Bill tongue-kissed me
When I was having a drooling
Contest outside with the boys.
Bill said to us, "I'm just cleaning
the drool from her face."
I flipped him off and he called in
My parents to tell them I was doing
Badly in school.
One day a boy vomited banana on
The school floor, and Bill licked it up.
He wasn't right in the head.
Now he runs a puppet shop in Montana.

DAPHNE

According to the June 16 *Daily Mail*,
A fifty-four-year-old woman went
To check on her garden & was swallowed
By a python. She was wearing
Brown pants & a dark red blouse
& was swallowed headfirst, her feet
Staying near the snake's mouth.
A dominatrix claimed that, sexually
Speaking, a man wants to kill
A woman & a woman wants
To eat a man.
The vagina is of course a mouth.
I dig my feet deep into the cold,
Wet, green grass under the
Tree. It's hot & dry everywhere in
Town but right here. I'm in an oasis
Of cool green surrounded
By endless drought & dust.
This tree has bulges as if
It swallowed something it is now digesting.
The bulges must be the result
Of a parasite & they are beautiful.
I burrow my feet down,
I put my hands on the tree.
My hair is leaves.

SANTA FE

Muhammad's daughter Fatima
Plunged her hands into the body
Of a slain enemy & made blood
Prints on a white cloth.
It became a flag.

In ancient Spain, pomegranate
Blossoms & Fatima's victory hands
Were worn around the necks
Of the Moorish horses.
The Spanish protected their
Conquistadors with flowers.

The Navajo squash blossom necklace
Worn all over my Santa Fe hometown
Is the horseshoe shape of
Fatima's bloody paws hanging in
Silver between tourists' breasts.

ALGERIA

You eat a songbird
From beginning to end.
You pierce your gums
With tiny ribs
For a squirt of her liquor
Down your throat.

Mitterrand hid his pleasure & his shame
Under a clean white napkin as
His own blood mixed with his last meal.

We are kept in the dark
To be tender & fat.
The ortolan bunting sings
A beautiful song &
Stains our teeth from behind.

LOVE

I write his name on my belly,
On my thighs, on my tits.
I fuck a ketchup bottle.
He whips me with his belt.
He spanks me with a cutting board.
He does it to me because I do it to myself.
Sometimes being sexy makes me shy.
Sometimes it makes me unbearably sad.

I have trained myself to be able to come
Without anyone or anything touching me.
Santa Teresa de Ávila said love is the
Only way to be purely ecstatic.
& love is the desire to please God.
Sometimes I want the man I love to
Literally devour me.

The little girl inside me is God.
The little girl inside me is a black-cloaked assassin.
God slashes to shit all of my ancestors.
I smell like flowers because
He loves me.

GRAMERCY PARK

The windows around Gramercy have eyes.
We look, they look back.
A brook cut through the swamp.
The Dutch called it *Krom Mesje*, little crooked knife.
A little body of water is a dagger, a bigger body is a kill.
The Dutch came for beavers & named us all to pieces.

Baghdad is a swamp of killing.
Gramercy is a kill two acres big.
Bombs lit the desert sky like flowers.
The Super Hornet pilot says, It's lovely,
The only part of the Iraqi girl you can see is her eyes.
It's absolutely the most exclusive park in the world.

The Turks stormed Baghdad &
Decimated the Byzantines.
The winners had better arrows.
Balls of ice fell on the losers.
Inside each ball was a flower.
The flowers in the ice balls looked like eyes.

When you live on Gramercy Park,
You get two keys.
The doorman keeps them both.

CLEANING

I love watching the cleaning woman
Wipe the cabinets in the kitchen.
She wipes the white doors with her
Yellow cloth and I get tingles down my back.
I want to make them dirty so
I can watch her clean them again.
Sometimes I clean them myself
But it doesn't give me pleasure.
I like to clean the toilet.
I put on blue rubber gloves and
Scrub off the faint glow of pink at the
Waterline as soon as it begins to form.
I scrub and flush and do it again.
Only good will come from this.

I dream of black widow
Spiders everywhere.
I catch them in glass jars and
Watch their bodies foam.

THE TURTLE

My mother's pleasures are children's
Pleasures in a grown woman.
She still has a favorite color.
She loves ponies; she loves cookies.
She loves talking about herself as a
Little girl loving ponies & loving cookies.
She still sneaks sugar treats.
As if she's not allowed.
In her own house, a grown woman,
Married to a man who doesn't care.
A woman who once had a beautiful face
Now looking more & more
Like a turtle, a turtle-faced woman
Sneaking chocolate from no one who cares.

PINK

George W made a painting & painted his toes pink
Like the meat I eat
& the color of my baby's penis.

The triangle, the British Empire & the *Financial Times*.
Daughters, gardens & assholes.
All good things are pink.

Pink like the jelly bean on Daddy Reagan's desk.
Pink like the icing on the doughnut Dad gave me
In a truck he called Ghost.

I vomit *that* pink on myself
& don't tell anyone
That I'm talking pink from my pink mouth.

PINKS

Pink is the scarlet
Worn by foxhunters
& a flower with jagged petals.
It's the sound made by a drop
& a wee peep of light.

Pink is manners &
The color of least
Resistance.
Studies show that pink
Calms the male &
Excites the female.
In color theory,
Pink means *unconditional love.*

Pink used to mean yellow.
The word *pink* originally
Meant a Dutch warship.

Pink is to puncture,
To pierce.
It means deluxe beauty
& a secret plan.

Prick, stab,
To wound with a bullet.
& it's the color of girls.

They have rooms in prison
Painted pink to make you think
About being good.

I peel off the
Pink of my room
Strip by strip.

Ink is inside of pink.
Pink means violence, indecency
& our smallest finger.
It's also the scissors
I use to scallop the
Cloth for my dress.

Women protesting femicide
Paint colored hands clamped
Over their mouths.

Death in Juárez is pink.
The crosses of the murdered
& missing are painted pink.
A slaughterhouse of girls.

PURPLE

The hands of the Roman
Purple dyer reeked of rotten fish.
Twelve thousand snails
Decimated for the trim
Of a royal robe.

It was the most desirable
Color on earth. Only
The most powerful
& wealthy could wear it.

The most prized of purples was
Like blackish clotted blood.

Blood brought to the
Surface of skin is purple.
By pleasure & by pain.
By love bites & by bruises.
I wear purple marks from
You on my eyes & hips.

TIERRA DEL FUEGO

Fires sprouted like tongues
Through the fog.
The Portuguese explorers saw
Them in the dark.
Fires in the Selk'nam canoes like
Tongues of light flickering in the night.
The Spanish & the Dutch made
Sure it stayed lonely.
They turned it into a blood-cold sea.

Patagonia means: *those of the large feet.*
The natives were tall, dressed in skins of seals.
Julius Popper was the savage
Who demanded two pounds sterling
Per pair of Selk'nam ears.
He & his men, the bounty hunters,
Killed them all.

Ferdinand Magellan got to name it.
Ptolemy drew Tierra del Fuego on a map.
In AD 800, al-Khwarizmi drew it too.
Darwin tagged & labeled it.
Margaret Thatcher stamped her name on it.

For a time, the only way to get from
New York to San Francisco was to scrape
Your ship's hull with Antarctic ice.

When I met María del Mar,
I don't know why I imagined her
Splayed out naked on a bed,
Like a dead bird.
Taut muscles in her fleshy body,
Parted lips, brown nipples.
I immediately desired her,
I immediately felt angry at her.

It was through her body, María del Mar,
Her thighs, María del Mar, that we were
Pushed beyond repair.
Going into the sea as one form
& coming out other.
My mouth on her neck,
Her pelvis on my waist.
Darwin tagged us.
María del Mar, my little ocean.
My mouth was too small to take her all in.

PICNIC WITH MOM

She goes off to look at birds.
I go for a shot in the dark
With room for cream.
I sneeze.
We eat apples
& throw stones into the water.
Westinghouse light bulbs make us look old.
Westinghouse blender makes us drunk.
I can't build a fire for shit;
I'm not a Girl Scout.
She is tall in wooden shoes.
I am a whore in heels.
I put her braid in my mouth
& bite down hard.

THE PONTE VECCHIO

The Ponte Vecchio was built
For butcher shops.
The river stitched with bridges
Ran with blood.
The only one Hitler spared,
From windows cut
Just for him to love the view.
The bridge of padlocked love.

In the shadow of the old bridge,
The statues glow in the dark.
Our room oversees
The grip of Pluto clamping
Deep into Proserpina's
Fleeing thigh, her fleshy hip.
My haunches are her haunches.
Be *mine* but I couldn't be yours enough.

Cosimo I de' Medici didn't want to walk
To work over the smell of blood.
So goldsmiths replaced the butchers.

CAPRICE

My mother confuses Topeka with Toledo.
My father confuses me with my mother.
Spain didn't conquer Kansas,
It conquered New Mexico.
Topeka means onion.
Toledo means sword of steel.
David & Goliath
Both have Caravaggio's face —
Victor & victim same.
I am from New Mexico,
My father is from Topeka.
I know how to be conquered & I go to Spain.
Maja doesn't know Kansas or Ohio.
She does know swords & onions.
She dresses, she undresses.
All of my violence is in the Prado.

SCHWARZHEIDE

Spain searched the New World
For the bodies of females,
Collected by the thousands and crushed
For a color only the rich could wear,
Because they were more valuable than gold.

The red stripes on the first American flag.
The red painted lips in Rubens and Vermeer.
The Redcoats, Russia's Imperial Guards
Were all cochineal insect red.

I want my mother to talk red
But she won't. When I dream about
Her, she has no breasts and no blood.
She opens her robe
And reveals a hollowed-out chest.
I split her head with a shovel,
But still she does not bleed.
The devil's made of shame.

Life is red, history is white.
It's a Luc Tuymans painting
Drained of color.
We see only the trees,
Not the death camp.

THE FORTUNE TELLER

Lying awake in the middle of the night.
What was done & wasn't done.
Things I don't like about people I love.
Origin stories & dress-up.
We look at paintings.
Face of the fortune teller,
Girl who's a thief.
I don't know exactly what I see when I look at you.

I caught you looking at Asian porn.
The pink cavern mouth of a teen
Tied & flayed.
Like Pontormo's Mary,
Eyes of pain & ecstatic same.
You like this, the pain & pleasure in girls.

De La Tour spent his life in the duchy of Lorraine.
Our bed smells of yeast & deer musk.
You woke up & said
You need paintings & champagne.
& to lick a girl with peasant curves.
You've selected me witness
For what was & wasn't done.
I am a thief,
Feed me.

SWEDISH BIRDS

The Swedish birds hung in our kitchen.
My brother & I broke them
With a ball & a stick by mistake.
Our Sámi mother screamed &
Crumpled in grief, then was gone.
Away looking for the fragments
Who forgot their own language, looking
Elsewhere for broken bodies to make more broken.
These bodies we make, these bodies we destroy.
Life makes life.
Death also does.

Andrea Yates drowned
Her five babies one by one
In the bathtub, then gently
Laid out their bodies
On her bed to make it look
Like they were sleeping.
But she wasn't trying to get
Away with it.

MOTHERS

Women in Japan used to wean
Their babies by painting their breasts black.
Hurricane clouds are black.
The earth is weaning us.

Sometimes I want the mother
Of the man I love to walk
In on us so she knows
He's mine and no longer hers.

My son asks me what it would be
Like if he were a scorpion, a
Shark or a black widow and
I had to give birth to these animals
And then give them my breast milk.

I think it's interesting that it's the
Size of our minds that makes
Childbirth so dangerous;
The bigness of our brains
Sometimes kills our mothers.

The Congolese rainforest is the
Wet, nurturing heart pumping

Oxygen for the world.
It's also where we got the radioactive stone
For the bombs on Nagasaki and Hiroshima.

I stand in the courtyard and look up
And see that the weather in the top of the trees
Is different from the weather down below.

THE END

The origin of *kicking the bucket*
Might be from the French *trébuchet*—
The name of a balance beam used to
Suspend animals for the slaughter.
In the throes of death, the pigs
Spasm & *kick the bucket*.

Or perhaps from the moment of Spanish death—
Estirar la pata—when the legs stretch out
& knock over the dish of holy
Water offered at the feet.

Or maybe from the goats on
The Island of Skyros—
Who, in rebellion, and/or self-sabotage,
Kick over their
Own pail of milk.

BABYLON

The Hittites razed Babylon.
It was the most important city in the world
& now it's completely gone.

The beams for the Empire State
Building were laid still warm.
The tower razed the sky.

Babylon means confusion.
The Tower of Confusion.
The Hanging Gardens of Confusion.
The sins of Confusion.

Wall Street is named for the wall
Built by slaves to keep the
African slaves from escaping.

The Persians drained the Euphrates
To sneak in & conquer Babylon.
All that's left of Babylon is a swampy
Pond. You can see it from the
Palace of Saddam Hussein.

If the scene of the crime
Is still warm, we return.

BOW

To render.
To retreat, swerve, decline.
To assume a crooked shape,
A coiled serpent.
A weapon for shooting arrows.
An inclination of the body in reverence.
To become a subject, to leave the stage.
Submission.

A painter is a rope
Tied to the bow of a boat.
The painter renders.
Frida said her trolley-car
Pain was nothing compared
To her Diego pain.

VOLTERRA

A day of prosecco & maps.
You inhaled the musk from my hair.
You drove my childhood curves;
I dressed in the part.

I rode shotgun in
Your dead father's Porsche.
The car he never lived
Long enough to drive.
The car he never could afford.

Tupac took us up to the hill town,
Bach fugues brought us down.
They say the first witch ever,
Daughter of the huntress Diana &
The Devil himself, was born
& cast her spells here. The church
Tortured her & stretched her
Out on a stretching frame.

You said you liked Rosso Fiorentino's
Deposition because it's so simple.
But the green & smiling god

Collapsing in the painting you need
Is actually the most complicated
Thing in the world.
The body is being removed from
That which defined it.

PINK

Pink is the Tuscan sunset.
Pink are the Vietnamese monk pates bobbing
Under Piero's True Cross.
Pink is plenty, pink is joy.

My pelvis is pink.
I wrap my pink legs
Around the man who calls me Cake.
Pink is bending over.
Pink is my darkness, clearly.

The fat dwarf in the Boboli garden
Has thick white spiderweb inside his mouth.
I use my mouth but not to speak.
The pink peonies are so
Heavy they're pulling
Down their own stalks.
This garden is astonishing.
The man who paints bouquets
Sits on the terrace & draws
The dying purple iris in the silver pitcher.
He paints & smokes & touches
His cock & looks at himself
In the window pane.

He drinks a bottle of champagne
& paints the background teal.
He doesn't know how to accurately capture
The reflections in the silver of the pitcher.
The lights twinkle pink in Fiesole.

He wears pink shirts.
He screams pink.
He pinks me so hard
I have scar tissue.
But, *In bed, it's theater*.

The landscape in Italy
Is all spoken for.
The pink man likes the word *whore*.
I drink Earl Grey tea with cream.
I am reminded that
The pink man likes obedience.
The Florentine moon is behind a fig leaf.
On the streets I am the girl repeated.
At home, I am exactly what he likes.
The flesh in paintings.
The word *pain* is in *painting*.
The wounds repaired
With mulberry tissue.
But from the side you can

Always still see the wounds
In the canvas like mouths.
The mouths in the paintings
Part like wounds.
The paintings
Are of the wounds
In the flesh.

I have two mouths & both are pink.
The wounds on Christ are female.
I swallow your pink entirely.
The lights twinkle pink in Fiesole.

Florence violently seized Fiesole,
& Rome bullied Florence.
The origin of the word
Bully is *lover.*
Florence is a *flowering sword.*

Rosso's green, deposed Christ.
The body being removed
From that which gave it power.
You like your girls the same.

You paint yourself
In a mirror looking

Up out of the sea.
An arrogance that only
A broken man can have.
Only a man who can't love
Can fuck me like that.

The sack of Rome,
The siege of Florence.
The lights twinkle pink in Fiesole.
Pink furls, pink buds.
Wet pink veiny hearts in spring.
Pink can mean so many things.

You are thrilled by the pink
Smear of hunted fox.
You are the lonely man who
Makes me cry, the only man.
Looking at yourself in the glass
You remind me.
The emptiness of pink.
I stand up too fast & all goes white.

You scream pink.
You pink me so hard
I have scar tissue.
We become our words. I didn't know

That what I said in bed is true.
I thought those words stayed in bed
But I became exactly what I said.
You said the words stayed in bed
But they got up & dressed me.

You grip the pink of my haunches
& tell me *not to do that again*—
But I do.
The pink of human kindness.
I can't belong to you enough.

It must be so nice
To be owned, you say.

The bodies of saints
Are broken apart
& stolen for worship.
You break apart
& I repair you.
You steal my body
& worship it.

It must feel so nice to
Belong to someone, you say.

You're gonna get it & I do.
Taking me apart to put
Yourself back together.
I starve.
But I gorge myself on Italy.
A mosaic cat eats a mosaic bird.
It's a wet & veiny spring.

I never want to leave the cloisters
Of San Marco. I stand & cry
& hold the walls.
My piety arouses you &
I cry harder.

I can't get out of the dark.
Pink is my darkness, clearly.
Something is rotten in Denmark.
Pink is thrilling & pink is chilling.
The purple marks
Of pink.

Soft, ripe, blue-veined cheese
& sparkling pink rosé.
The owls, the hooded crows.
I make a list of birds.
I make a painting trophy list.

Paintings are like swords
Poking through my numb.

I take your words & put them
In my body. The more
I speak pink the pinker
I become.

Orto in Italian is *garden*.
In Spanish, it's *asshole*.
That about sums it up,
You say.

The goddess of war is
The goddess of poetry.
They both spill blood
Pink & red.

Marks on bodies,
Marks on church walls,
Painted marks on wood.
The purple mark down on my back.
The angry pink man
Who makes me purple.

You remind me that you like the word *whore*.
The landscape in Italy is all spoken for.
I drink Earl Grey tea with cream.
I am reminded.
The pink man likes obedience.

Florence is a flower.
The tourists sparkle.
David got pinked, but
He pinked back.

You broke apart & I restored you.
You broke my heart & I adored you.

You're very pink & sorry.
You make that clearly pink.
You are the pink man who loves
Your pink to death.

I swallow your pink entirely.

Pecorino, liver, squash blossoms, wine.
Fried sage, anchovies,
Orange bruised fruits, orange fennel
Salad & fresh pea soup.

I eat freshly born lamb
Intestine, full still from the
Ewe's warm milk.
I use my mouth to eat but not to speak.

The man painting bouquets
Smokes red cigarettes.
Bored if it isn't about sex,
Bored if it isn't about death.

My fingers stained black from artichokes.
My neck is sore from where you choked me.

Lord, please increase my bewilderment.
The god of ecstasy is also the god of rage.
I climb inside you &
You scream me born.

Florence is the birthplace of
The vanishing point.